CHILLY

the very warm-blooded
Polar Bear

My favorite forms of literature are found in the Short Story and Poetry. As a Writer and Editor I can't seem to get away from these two forms. I find great expression in both of them. Join me here!

"...the short story can be read quickly in one sitting; it does not require careful perusal or a second reading to understand it, as might a poem.

"The modern short story first came into vogue with the growth of journalism, resulting in its publication in all types of magazines and journals. While the short story first became popular in the United States of America as an effort to create a distinct form of American literature separate from European styles, its popularity quickly grew in Europe." Anon.

A goal I have in life is to return the Poem to its noble place among literatures best read storytelling that will make sense the first time through. Poems should NEVER leave a person scratching their head in wonder. We have been duped in our society to believe that a good poem should tease our minds, and make us feel intellectually inferior to writers of the poetic lines.

Sorry, not buying it and I never have. You know things have gotten out of hand when people cringe when they hear a poet is going to do a reading. That is just criminal. The POEM should be a delight to read, to listen too, and to simply enjoy, making for a better day for everyone. The scratching of the head must stop. Most forms of writing in a book, magazine, or trade journal, should be understandable and not after reading the piece a dozen times.

A new story headed your way; I hope
it warms you up. It's still cold here,
waiting for Spring. This tale was
penned March 27th, 2013.

Cheers, Don

Chilly
the very warm blooded Polar Bear

I have two problems to deal with. One, I am cold all the time and I like living indoors, or where the temps are at least 70 degrees; plus, if you haven't noticed, I can communicate. That's why I'm here.

When I was small, I began uttering tiny noises that bears don't usually make. Before long, words began to form, and my parents got scared. They were afraid for my siblings. The sound of a human around could spell serious trouble.

I was made to leave our den, and had to find my own way in the world. I headed south away from this frigid world I was born into. I'd heard stories that temperatures were dropping across the globe, and this actually made me happy. Of course, my parents thought I was crazy, all wrapped up in my three or four blankets.

They let me take my blankets with me as I left. I figured I would never see them again, so I gave each a warm hug as I headed out the door. I hated ice, and I was sure I'd never want to come back to this place, though it held some great childhood memories.

Father tried to hide his tears. When I hugged him, he turned his head away so as not to let me see him shedding any. Mother wouldn't let go for a long time, then she ran into Father's paws, and hid her face in his deep fur.

The sooner I got away from here the better. I was choking up too; after all, I'm not totally insensitive. Soon I was miles away from my birthplace, and headed toward my new mission in life; whatever that was. I had found an old compass that a sailor left behind, and I used it to navigate my heading. I knew I had to follow the S-arrow.

After a terribly long trek over snowy mountains and deep valleys, I was getting really tired. I sensed I was nearing my new home. By now I was carrying my blankets; the warm breezes swirled all around me. I decided then and there to keep them, no matter how hot things got. They would serve as a reminder of my home away from home.

I was sure my family probably missed me by now. But I was left with no choice. I couldn't live there anymore, and I wasn't sure I belonged here either.

TIME PASSES...

I needed a new place and purpose in my life. All of my energies of thought had to go into this. The world I am now embarking on will be just as difficult, if not more so. People had never seen a talking bear. Yes, there were dancing bears aplenty, but nothing quite like me. I almost turned around to go back, having second thoughts, as I faced this new world.

I knew that I had a right to be me; to be exactly who I was, though I was different than most everyone else. Suddenly, I saw a sign on a window in town that was calling for circus acts. Maybe I could be one of the curio shows. There were bearded ladies, clowns, elephants, and a whole host of other oddities for folks to see and be entertained by.

It dawned on me that I could read to the children. I used to tell stories to my siblings as they fell asleep. Even though none of them understood the language as I did, they somehow were charmed by my voice. Could human kids enjoy my stories as much as my own family members?

"Mom, look at the bear. He's not in his cage; let's run for it."

The circus owner spied me and shot me twice with some sort of dart gun. I started feeling tired, and then I must have passed out. When I woke up, I found myself in a large animal cage. There were fish in a bowl, probably for me. I was sure I was gonna like this place.

I overheard two circus performers talking about me. "Jack, what does the owner want with an old bear, anyway?"

"I don't think he is that old. He looks pretty young to me. Maybe he can get the bear to do a special routine."

I wanted to shout, "Wait until you catch my act."

The owner then showed up at my cage. "Now let's have a look at what we've got here. You are such a beautiful bear. I wish I knew where you came from."

"Try the Northern region of Alaska! I remembered the sign posts where I once lived."

The owner nearly fell over in shock. It took a minute before he caught his breath. "Folks, we got ourselves a talking bear, an intelligent one. This fellow may have just saved our circus from extinction. We have not been able to make our payroll budget for several months now.

"With this new act we are assured of a packed house every night, and folks will travel any distance to witness what we just did. Everyone will say this is not possible, and then they will come to see it for themselves. Get a room ready for Chilly, our new employee."

"But boss, he's a wild bear!"

"He's the friendliest wild bear I've yet to come across. Get his room ready! Are you deaf?"

"No, sir. Right away!"

"So Chilly, I hope you like fish for dinner?" No one had ever addressed me before; much less given me a name.

I sat on the ground with my head and paws placed deeply into my lap. I was crying. I'd never felt like I ever belonged anywhere. My own forsook me; not truly understanding my situation. Here in this new world; I had found my resting place. No more wandering, and I would never want for friends again. This was just what the doctor ordered for the circus and for me.

UPDATE: Chilly was returned to his family up North for two weeks of **R & R** each year, while he always had a spot with his new circus family.
Other books to grace your library shelves.

A fun poem about Global Warming I though fit well with our story about "Chilly"and published at Dead Mule Poetry.

Donald Ford – "Chill Factor"
Chill Factor (Published Dec. 2010)

The world they say is getting warmer
Polar Bears are quite upset
No more ice in lemonade
I won't drink soda that's just wet

Gone will be the snow and snowman
Ice cream on a stick would fall
Everything in life would melt
It won't be any fun at all

Where is Mr. Chilling Frost?
It's not that I despise the heat
We really need Sir Cold North Wind
And Old Man Winter on his seat

Do a rain dance, it won't help
Temperatures are rising fast
In our dreams we'll wish for you
We need you, Mister Icy Blast

Connect the Dots

by Mr. Don G. Ford

In the last seven years I have been working on short stories; a plethora of them. I have decided to compile stories for the reader along various topics. This happens to be stories that are all fiction for the most part. I hope you find this selection of tales to be entertaining and worth what you invested in...

Publication Date: February 22, 2013

List Price: $7.99

Tree With the Money on it

by Mr. Don G. Ford

CreateSpace Store / BOOK

Every reader should be grabbing for this book. Times are tough, and having a money tree in the back yard could spell good times for all. See for yourself. This was created with the younger reader in mind, but parents and grandparents will want to have a look. This could go nicely beside the child's bed for a...

Publication Date: June 26, 2013

List Price: $5.99

Mirrored Self

by Mr. Don G. Ford

CreateSpace Store / BOOK

The mind will take us on an unusual journey here. The subject matter has been done to death, but this story puts a new twist on it. This tale is told with three characters, and by the end of it, you will see why three really is an irritation, and two will do rather nicely. If you enjoy a good Twilight Zone...

Publication Date: May 14, 2013

List Price: $4.99

Clay Pond - Lady Bugley

by Mr. Don G. Ford

CreateSpace Store / BOOK

Clay Pond is an adventure more than just a story. You will meet new friends here that you will want to keep forever. They will become as much a part of your life once you become involved in their lives. Once you enter Clay Pond, you will find a place you can return to at different times where you can relax; a...

Publication Date: June 27, 2013

List Price: $5.99

Funny Business

by Mr. Don G. Ford

The purpose of this compilation of short
stories, vignettes, and poems is to turn a few
smiles right side up. You'll run into spiders,
ghosts and even the little "Fly on the Wall". It's
all in fun and for everyone's reading pleasure.
If you have your boots on, jump right in. Every
chapter here is a...

Publication Date: March 28, 2013

List Price: $7.99

Nightfall Horror Anthology

by Mr. Don G. Ford

CreateSpace Store / BOOK

I attempt to write in every genre; horror is no exception. Even though I teach classes in Creative Writing and Writing For Publication, I enjoy putting on a fright show from time to time. Every door you open here may not creak, but I'd still be watching my back if I were you. I'm not here to scare people; it...

Publication Date: June 14, 2013

List Price: $7.99

Guess Who's Hiding at the Alphabet ZOO

by Mr. Don G. Ford

CreateSpace Store / BOOK

Life is all about variety, and no where is that truer than in the animal kingdom. There are different kinds of dogs, horses, fish, rabbits; you name it. This book will take you into the lives of many of those animals. If you didn't care before, or know that you should, remember that many of these creatures...

Publication Date: June 4, 2013

List Price: $10.99

The Great Migration

by Mr. Don G. Ford

If this story is received in the way I hope, it should be easy to see it on the large screen of the mind. It is my hope to drop the reader into the action and make them feel like they are there experiencing it each step of the way. I hope you will care about each character and their role in this adventure as...

Publication Date: April 1, 2013

List Price: $6.99

Heaven on the Line

by Mr. Don G. Ford

CreateSpace Store / BOOK

What if you were handed a phone number and it was God's number. How would you respond? In our stories the reader will see how other's responded to this news. When the towers went down, the last I heard was my son was going to be in one of the towers for breakfast with a friend. All day long his mother and I...

Publication Date: May 26, 2013

List Price: $6.99

No Such Animal as Writer's Block

by Mr. Don G. Ford

CreateSpace Store / BOOK

This book will finally do away with 'Writer's Block'; a DIRTY WORD in the world of literature. The treatment here covers various aspects of what slows or even stops a writer in his attempt to pen his pieces; more importantly, his ability to keep the ink flowing from one page to the next. There is substance...

Publication Date: May 27, 2013

List Price: $7.99

Floyd the Dog Story Book Commemorative

by Mr. Don G. Ford

CreateSpace Store / BOOK

Here is the new Book that I would love you to have a look at. The cover says it all. Michael St. John, Publisher of "Floyd the Dog", a Portuguese Book Club, has accepted so many of my stories that it only makes sense to honor him in this way. There's something in these tales for everyone. You can take this...

Publication Date: June 20, 2013

List Price: $19.99

www.ingramcontent.com/pod-product-compliance
Lightning Source LLC
Chambersburg PA
CBHW030553290526
45786CB00004B/2006